Perpignan Travel Guide 2024

Experience the Warmth of Southern France: A Traveler's Guide to Perpignan's Hidden Gems

ALEXANDER PAUL

Copyright© 2024 ALEXANDER PAUL

All rights reserved.
No part of this book may be reproduced, stored in a retrieval system, or transmitted in any form or by any means, electronic, mechanical, photocopying, recording, or otherwise, without the prior written permission of the publisher.
Unauthorized reproduction of this book, or parts thereof, is prohibited by law and may result in legal action.

Table of Contents

Chapter 1: Introduction   **10**
- Welcome to Perpignan   10
- Historical Overview   12
- Highlights of 2024   14
  - Cultural Festivals   14
  - New Attractions   15
  - Gastronomic Delights   15
  - Sporting Events   15
  - Sustainable Initiatives   16
  - Art and Exhibitions   16
  - Music and Nightlife   17
  - Historical Reenactments   17
  - Local Markets   17
  - Wellness and Relaxation   18

Chapter 2: Getting There and Around   **19**
- By Air   20
  - Perpignan–Rivesaltes Airport   21
  - Getting from the Airport to the City Center   21
  - Alternative Airports   22
- By Train   22
  - Perpignan Train Station   23
  - Regional Trains (TER)   24
- By Car   24
  - Major Highways   25
  - Parking in Perpignan   26
- Public Transportation Options   27

Bike Sharing	28
Taxis and Ride-Sharing	28
Exploring Beyond Perpignan	29
Chapter 3: Accommodation	**31**
Luxury Hotels	32
La Villa Duflot	32
Hôtel de la Loge	33
Best Western Plus Hôtel Windsor	34
Boutique Hotels	34
Casa 9 Hôtel	34
Hôtel La Fauceille	35
Le Mas des Arcades	35
Budget Stays	35
Hôtel Mondial	36
Ibis Budget Perpignan Centre Méditerranée	36
Hôtel Paris-Barcelone	37
Family-Friendly Options	38
Novotel Suites Perpignan Mediterranée	38
Appart'City Perpignan Centre Gare	39
Camping Les Criques de Porteils	39
Unique Lodging: Villas and B&Bs	40
Villa Duflot Hôtel & Spa	40
Domaine de Nidolères	40
Château La Tour Apollinaire	40
Mas Latour Lavail	40
Gîtes du Mas Julianas	41
Chapter 4: Major Attractions	**43**
Palais des Rois de Majorque	43
Historical Significance	44

Architectural Features	44
Visitor Experience	44
Perpignan Cathedral	45
Historical Background	46
Architectural Highlights	46
Visitor Experience	47
Le Castillet	47
Historical Importance	47
Architectural Features	49
Visitor Experience	49
Jardin de la Miranda	49
Overview	49
Features	52
Visitor Experience	52
Musée d'art Hyacinthe Rigaud	52
Historical Background	53
Collections and Exhibits	53
Visitor Experience	53
Special Exhibitions	54
Museum Amenities	54
Chapter 5: Exploring Neighborhoods	**55**
The Historic Center	56
Overview	56
Key Attractions	57
Saint-Jacques	58
Overview	58
Key Attractions	60
Cultural Diversity	60
Les Remparts	61

Overview	61
Key Attractions	62
La Gare District	63
Overview	63
Key Attractions	65
Dining and Shopping	65
Modern Conveniences	66
Chapter 6: Cultural Experiences	**66**
Local Festivals and Events	67
La Sanch Procession	67
Les Jeudis de Perpignan	68
Visa pour l'Image	70
Fête de la Saint-Jean	70
Theatre and Performances	71
Théâtre de l'Archipel	71
Le Médiator	72
Théâtre Municipal	73
Art Galleries and Exhibitions	73
Musée d'art Hyacinthe Rigaud	73
Traditional Music and Dance	75
Sardana	75
Cobla Music	76
Rumba Catalana	76
Chapter 7: Outdoor Adventures	**77**
Hiking and Nature Trails	79
Les Orgues d'Ille-sur-Têt	79
Pic du Canigou	81
La Massane	82
Beaches and Water Activities	83

Canet-en-Roussillon	83
Collioure	85
Cycling Routes	85
Voie Verte	85
Parks and Gardens	87
Jardin de la Miranda	87
Chapter 8: Culinary Delights	**88**
Traditional Catalan Cuisine	90
Fruits de Mer	90
Escudella i Carn d'Olla	91
Crema Catalana	92
Top Restaurants	93
Le Divil	93
La Galinette	94
L'Alchimiste	94
Street Food and Markets	94
Place de la République Market	94
Food Trucks and Stands	95
Local Wineries and Vineyards	96
Domaine Lafage	96
Domaine de Rombeau	97
Mas Janeil	97
Chapter 9: Shopping Experiences	**98**
Local Markets	99
Shopping Streets and Malls	101
Unique Souvenirs	102
Artisan Shops	102
Chapter 10: Day Trips	**104**
Collioure	105

Overview	105
Céret	108
Overview	108
Castelnou	109
Overview	109
The Pyrenees Mountains	110
Overview	110
Chapter 11: Practical Information	**112**
Currency and Money Matters	112
Language Tips	113
Safety and Health	113
Internet and Connectivity	113
Emergency Contacts	114
Chapter 12: Travel Tips	**115**
Best Times to Visit	116
Essential Packing List	117
Eco-Friendly Travel Practices	118
Local Etiquette	119
Chapter 13: Conclusion	**121**
Summary of Perpignan's Highlights	121
Tips for a Memorable Visit	123
Farewell and Future Visits	124
Chapter 14: Appendix	**124**
Maps of Perpignan	125
Useful Phrases in French and Catalan	125
Recommended Reading and Resources	127
Index	128

Chapter 1: Introduction

Welcome to Perpignan

Nestled in the heart of the Pyrénées-Orientales department in southern France, Perpignan is a vibrant city that seamlessly blends rich history with modern charm. Located near the

Mediterranean coast and the Spanish border, Perpignan is a gateway to the beauty and culture of both France and Catalonia. Known for its sunny climate, colourful streets, and welcoming locals, this city offers a unique blend of French and Catalan influences, making it a captivating destination for travellers.

Perpignan is a city that invites exploration. Whether you're wandering through its narrow medieval streets, relaxing in its lush gardens, or savouring its delectable cuisine, there's something here for everyone. This guide aims to provide you with all the practical information you need to make the most of your visit, from the best places to stay and eat to the must-see attractions and hidden gems.

Historical Overview

Perpignan's history is as rich and varied as its cultural
tapestry. Founded by the Romans in the 2nd century BC, the

city has seen a succession of rulers and influences over the centuries. Its strategic location made it a valuable prize for various powers, including the Visigoths, the Moors, and the Carolingians.

In the 13th century, Perpignan became the capital of the Kingdom of Majorca, and this period left a significant architectural legacy in the city. The impressive Palais des Rois de Majorque, or Palace of the Kings of Majorca, is a testament to this era, showcasing Gothic architecture and offering stunning views of the surrounding area.

By the 17th century, Perpignan was incorporated into France following the Treaty of the Pyrenees in 1659. This marked a new chapter in the city's history, blending French and Catalan cultures. Today, you can see this unique fusion in everything from the local language and traditions to the cuisine and festivals.

Highlights of 2024

Perpignan in 2024 promises to be an exciting year with a host of events, new attractions, and cultural activities that highlight the city's vibrant spirit. Here are some highlights you won't want to miss:

Cultural Festivals

Perpignan is known for its lively festivals, and 2024 is no exception. The city's calendar is packed with events celebrating its rich cultural heritage. The annual Sant Joan Festival in June is a spectacular celebration of Catalan traditions, featuring bonfires, fireworks, and street parades. Additionally, the Visa pour l'Image, one of the world's leading photojournalism festivals, will take place in September, attracting photographers and enthusiasts from around the globe.

New Attractions

In 2024, Perpignan will unveil several new attractions that promise to enhance the visitor experience. The long-awaited opening of the Musée d'Art Moderne is set to be a highlight. This museum will showcase contemporary art from both local and international artists, adding a modern touch to the city's rich cultural landscape. Additionally, the Jardin des Plantes, a botanical garden featuring a wide variety of Mediterranean plants, will offer a serene escape for nature lovers.

Gastronomic Delights

Perpignan's culinary scene is evolving, with new restaurants and food markets enhancing the city's reputation as a gastronomic destination. The local cuisine, a delightful blend of French and Catalan flavours, will be showcased in the annual Perpignan Food Festival. Scheduled for October 2024, this event will bring together top chefs, local producers, and food enthusiasts for a celebration of regional dishes and innovative culinary creations.

Sporting Events

Sports enthusiasts will find plenty to enjoy in Perpignan in 2024. The city is home to the USA Perpignan rugby team, and attending one of their matches at the Stade Aimé Giral is a must for fans of the sport. Additionally, the Tour de France will pass through Perpignan in July, offering a thrilling opportunity to witness one of the world's most famous cycling races up close.

Sustainable Initiatives

Perpignan is committed to sustainability and has introduced several green initiatives that visitors can appreciate. The city has expanded its network of bike paths, making it easier than ever to explore on two wheels. Additionally, several new eco-friendly accommodations have opened, offering sustainable options for environmentally conscious travellers.

Art and Exhibitions

Perpignan's art scene continues to thrive, with numerous exhibitions and galleries to explore. The Musée d'art Hyacinthe Rigaud, known for its extensive collection of paintings, sculptures, and decorative arts, will host a special exhibition dedicated to the works of Salvador Dalí, celebrating the artist's connection to the region. This exhibition will run from April to September 2024 and is expected to draw art lovers from around the world.

Music and Nightlife

The music scene in Perpignan is diverse and vibrant, with something for everyone. In 2024, the Festival Jazzèbre will return, bringing world-class jazz musicians to various venues across the city. This festival, held in October, is a highlight of the city's cultural calendar. For those looking to experience the local nightlife, the Rue des Augustins is the place to be, with its lively bars, clubs, and music venues entertaining late into the night.

Historical Reenactments

One of the most unique experiences in Perpignan is the annual historical reenactment of the Battle of Perpignan. Held in August, this event brings the past to life with costumed actors, mock battles, and medieval markets. It's a fantastic way to learn about the city's history while enjoying a fun and engaging spectacle.

Local Markets

No visit to Perpignan would be complete without exploring its vibrant local markets. The Marché de la République is a bustling market where you can find fresh produce, local cheeses, and handmade crafts. In 2024, a new market focusing on organic and sustainable products will open in the Saint-Jacques neighbourhood, offering visitors a chance to discover the best of the region's natural bounty.

Wellness and Relaxation

For those seeking relaxation, Perpignan offers several wellness options. The newly opened Thermes de Perpignan, a luxurious thermal spa, provides a range of treatments and therapies designed to rejuvenate the body and mind. Additionally, the city's beautiful parks and gardens offer peaceful retreats where you can unwind and enjoy the Mediterranean climate.

In conclusion, Perpignan in 2024 is a city brimming with energy, culture, and new experiences. Whether you're a history buff, a food lover, an art enthusiast, or simply looking for a beautiful place to relax, Perpignan has something to offer. This guide will help you navigate the city's many attractions and make the most of your visit. Welcome to Perpignan – a city where the past meets the present, and every corner has a story to tell.

Chapter 2: Getting There and Around

Perpignan, located in the southern part of France, is easily accessible from various parts of the world. This chapter will guide you on the best ways to get to Perpignan and how to navigate the city once you arrive.

By Air

Perpignan–Rivesaltes Airport

The Perpignan–Rivesaltes Airport (PGF) is the primary airport serving the city. Situated approximately 5 kilometres north of the city centre, it offers both domestic and international flights. Major airlines like Air France, Ryanair, and EasyJet operate regular flights to and from key European cities such as Paris, London, and Brussels.

Getting from the Airport to the City Center

Upon arrival at Perpignan–Rivesaltes Airport, you have several options to reach the city centre:

- Taxi: Taxis are readily available outside the terminal. A ride to the city centre typically takes about 15 minutes and costs around €15-€20, depending on traffic.
- Shuttle Bus: The airport shuttle bus, Line 7, connects the airport to the city centre and the central bus station. The journey takes approximately 30 minutes, with buses running every hour.
- Car Rental: Several car rental companies operate at the airport, including Hertz, Avis, and Europcar. Renting a car offers the flexibility to explore the surrounding region at your own pace.

Alternative Airports

For more flight options, consider nearby airports such as Girona-Costa Brava Airport (GRO) in Spain and Toulouse-Blagnac Airport (TLS) in France. Both are within a few hours' drive of Perpignan and offer a wider range of international flights.

By Train

Perpignan Train Station

Perpignan's train station, known as Gare de Perpignan, is a major hub in the region, offering excellent connectivity to various parts of France and beyond. The station is located within walking distance of the city centre, making it a convenient arrival point for travellers.

High-Speed Trains (TGV)
The TGV (Train à Grande Vitesse) services connect Perpignan with several major cities in France:

- Paris: Direct TGV services link Perpignan with Paris Gare de Lyon in about 5 hours. These trains are fast, comfortable, and equipped with amenities like Wi-Fi and dining options.
- Barcelona: High-speed trains also connect Perpignan with Barcelona in around 1 hour and 20 minutes, providing a seamless connection between France and Spain.
- Toulouse and Marseille: Regular TGV services run between Perpignan and cities like Toulouse (2 hours) and Marseille (4 hours), making it easy to explore more of southern France.

Regional Trains (TER)

The regional TER trains connect Perpignan with smaller towns and cities within the Occitanie region. These trains are ideal for day trips and exploring the local area. Popular destinations include Narbonne, Carcassonne, and Collioure.

Getting from the Train Station to Your Destination

From Gare de Perpignan, you can reach your accommodation or other destinations in the city by:

- Taxi: Taxi are available outside the station, providing a quick and convenient way to reach your destination.
- Bus: Several bus lines operate from the station, offering connections to various parts of the city and surrounding areas.

- Walking: Many hotels and attractions are within walking distance of the station, especially if you are staying in the city centre.

By Car

Driving to Perpignan offers the freedom to explore the region at your own pace. The city is well-connected by a network of highways, making it accessible from various parts of France and neighbouring countries.

Major Highways

- A9 Motorway: The A9 motorway, also known as La Languedocienne, runs from Orange in southeastern France to the Spanish border. It connects Perpignan with major cities like Montpellier, Nîmes, and Barcelona.

24

- D900 Road: This road provides a direct route from Perpignan to the Mediterranean coast and is a scenic drive, especially in the summer months.

Parking in Perpignan

Finding parking in Perpignan is generally straightforward, with several options available:

- Street Parking: Street parking is available throughout the city, with metered spaces in the city centre. Pay attention to parking signs and restrictions to avoid fines.
- Parking Garages: There are several parking garages in the city centre, such as the Parking République and Parking Catalogne. These provide secure, covered parking and are convenient for accessing major attractions.
- Park and Ride: For long-term parking, consider using the park-and-ride facilities located on the outskirts of the city. These offer affordable parking with easy access to public transportation into the city centre.

Renting a Car

Car rental is a popular option for visitors looking to explore beyond Perpignan. Major rental companies like Hertz, Avis, and Enterprise operate in the city. It's advisable to book in advance, especially during peak travel seasons, to ensure availability and secure the best rates.

Public Transportation Options

Perpignan boasts an efficient and user-friendly public transportation system, making it easy to get around the city without a car.

Bus Services

The bus network in Perpignan is operated by Sankéo, offering extensive coverage of the city and its suburbs. Here are some key details:

- Routes: Numerous bus lines connect the city centre with residential neighbourhoods, shopping districts, and tourist attractions.
- Frequencies: Buses generally run every 10-20 minutes during peak hours and every 30 minutes during off-peak times.

- Tickets: Tickets can be purchased at bus stops, online, or directly from the driver. A single ticket costs around €1.30, and day passes are available for unlimited travel within a day.

Bike Sharing

Perpignan has embraced eco-friendly transportation with its bike-sharing program, BIP (Bicycle in Perpignan). Here's what you need to know:

- Stations: There are numerous bike stations throughout the city, especially near major attractions and transport hubs.
- Pricing: Bikes can be rented by the hour or with a daily pass, offering a cost-effective and healthy way to explore the city.
- Availability: BIP bikes are available 24/7, making them a convenient option for both short trips and longer excursions.

Taxis and Ride-Sharing

Taxis and ride-sharing services like Uber are readily available in Perpignan. Taxis can be hailed on the street, found at designated taxi stands, or booked in advance by phone or online. Ride-sharing services offer an alternative, often at a lower cost, and can be booked via mobile apps.

Walking

Perpignan is a compact and walkable city, with many of its attractions located within a short distance of each other. Walking is an excellent way to soak up the city's atmosphere, discover hidden gems, and enjoy the local architecture and street life.

Exploring Beyond Perpignan

If you plan to explore the surrounding region, consider these options:

- Regional Trains: TER trains provide connections to nearby towns and cities, making day trips convenient.
- Bus Services: Regional bus services connect Perpignan with coastal towns, mountain villages, and other points of interest in the Pyrénées-Orientales region.
- Car Rentals: For maximum flexibility, renting a car allows you to venture further afield and explore the scenic countryside, charming villages, and coastal areas at your own pace.

In summary, getting to Perpignan and navigating the city is straightforward, whether you prefer flying, taking the train, driving, or using public transportation. This accessibility, combined with the city's compact layout and efficient transport options, ensures that you can easily explore all that Perpignan and its surrounding region have to offer.

Chapter 3: Accommodation

Perpignan offers a wide range of accommodations to suit every taste and budget. Whether you're looking for luxury, charm, affordability, family-friendly options, or unique lodging experiences, you'll find the perfect place to stay in this vibrant city. This chapter will guide you through the best options available to make your stay comfortable and memorable.

Luxury Hotels

La Villa Duflot

La Villa Duflot is a prestigious 4-star hotel located just a few minutes from the city centre. Set in a lush Mediterranean garden, this hotel offers a tranquil escape with top-notch amenities. Guests can enjoy spacious rooms decorated in a contemporary style, a large outdoor pool, and an on-site gourmet restaurant serving French and Catalan cuisine. The hotel also features a spa and wellness centre, providing a range of treatments to help you unwind.

Hôtel de la Loge

Situated in the heart of Perpignan's historic centre, Hôtel de la Loge offers luxury and convenience in equal measure. This boutique 4-star hotel is housed in a beautifully restored 18th-century building, blending historic charm with modern comforts. Each room is elegantly decorated and equipped with high-end amenities. The hotel's central location makes it an ideal base for exploring Perpignan's attractions, restaurants, and shops.

Best Western Plus Hôtel Windsor

Located near the Palais des Congrès, the Best Western Plus Hôtel Windsor offers luxury accommodations with panoramic views of the city. This modern 4-star hotel features stylish rooms with contemporary decor, a fitness centre, and a rooftop terrace where guests can enjoy breakfast with a view. The hotel's prime location provides easy access to Perpignan's main sights and business district.

Boutique Hotels

Casa 9 Hôtel

For those seeking a unique and intimate experience, Casa 9 Hôtel is a charming boutique hotel located in the nearby village of Thuir, just a short drive from Perpignan. Set in a historic 13th-century building, this hotel offers a serene and romantic atmosphere. Each room is individually decorated with antique furnishings and modern touches. Guests can relax by the outdoor pool, stroll through the beautifully landscaped gardens, and enjoy breakfast on the terrace.

Hôtel La Fauceille

Hôtel La Fauceille is a boutique hotel that combines modern design with a warm, welcoming ambience. Located on the outskirts of Perpignan, this 4-star hotel offers stylish rooms with private balconies, an outdoor pool, and a gourmet restaurant serving innovative Mediterranean cuisine. The hotel's personalized service and tranquil setting make it a perfect choice for couples and solo travellers looking for a relaxing getaway.

Le Mas des Arcades

Le Mas des Arcades is a charming boutique hotel situated in a quiet residential area, offering a peaceful retreat from the bustling city centre. This 3-star hotel features comfortable rooms with rustic decor, an outdoor pool, and a lush garden where guests can unwind. The on-site restaurant serves traditional Catalan dishes, and the friendly staff provides personalized service to ensure a pleasant stay.

Budget Stays

Hôtel Mondial

Hôtel Mondial is a budget-friendly option located in the heart of Perpignan, close to the train station and major attractions. This 2-star hotel offers simple yet comfortable rooms with all the basic amenities needed for a pleasant stay. The hotel's central location makes it an ideal choice for travellers looking to explore the city on foot without breaking the bank.

Ibis Budget Perpignan Centre Méditerranée

For travellers on a budget, the Ibis Budget Perpignan Centre Méditerranée offers affordable and convenient accommodations. Located within walking distance of the city centre, this 2-star hotel features clean and functional rooms with modern amenities. Guests can enjoy a buffet breakfast each morning and take advantage of the hotel's 24-hour reception and free Wi-Fi.

Hôtel Paris-Barcelone

Hôtel Paris-Barcelone is another excellent budget option, conveniently situated near the train station. This 2-star hotel offers cosy rooms with essential amenities, making it a comfortable base for exploring Perpignan. The friendly staff provides helpful recommendations on local attractions and dining options, ensuring guests have an enjoyable stay.

Family-Friendly Options

Novotel Suites Perpignan Mediterranée

Novotel Suites Perpignan Mediterranée is an ideal choice for families, offering spacious suites that can accommodate up to four people. Located in the city centre, this 4-star hotel features modern amenities, including a fitness centre, a children's play area, and an on-site restaurant with a kid-friendly menu. The hotel's convenient location allows families to easily explore Perpignan's attractions, shops, and restaurants.

Appart'City Perpignan Centre Gare

For families seeking more space and the convenience of self-catering facilities, Appart'City Perpignan Centre Gare offers serviced apartments with fully equipped kitchens. Located near the train station, this 3-star property provides easy access to the city centre and surrounding areas. The apartments are spacious and comfortable, with amenities such as free Wi-Fi, laundry facilities, and a breakfast service.

Camping Les Criques de Porteils

For a unique family-friendly experience, consider staying at Camping Les Criques de Porteils, located just outside Perpignan in the picturesque town of Argelès-sur-Mer. This campsite offers a range of accommodation options, including mobile homes and bungalows, with direct access to the beach. The site features numerous amenities, such as swimming pools, sports facilities, a kids' club, and evening entertainment, ensuring a fun-filled stay for the whole family.

Unique Lodging: Villas and B&Bs

Villa Duflot Hôtel & Spa

Villa Duflot Hôtel & Spa is a luxurious villa-style hotel located just outside Perpignan. Set in a tranquil park, this 4-star property offers elegant rooms and suites with private terraces, an outdoor pool, and a spa offering a range of treatments. The hotel's restaurant serves gourmet cuisine in a stylish setting, and the lush gardens provide a peaceful escape from the city.

Domaine de Nidolères

For a unique and charming experience, consider staying at Domaine de Nidolères, a family-run B&B located in the countryside near Perpignan. This historic property offers comfortable rooms with rustic decor, surrounded by vineyards and olive groves. Guests can enjoy a homemade breakfast each morning, featuring local products, and relax by the outdoor pool. The friendly hosts provide a warm welcome and offer insights into the local area.

Château La Tour Apollinaire

Château La Tour Apollinaire is a stunning 19th-century mansion offering unique and luxurious accommodations. Located in a quiet residential area, this boutique B&B features individually decorated rooms and suites with antique furnishings and modern amenities. Guests can relax in the beautifully landscaped gardens, take a dip in the outdoor pool, and enjoy a delicious breakfast each morning. The château's elegant and romantic ambience makes it a perfect choice for couples.

Mas Latour Lavail

Mas Latour Lavail is a beautifully restored 16th-century farmhouse offering a unique lodging experience. Located on the outskirts of Perpignan, this B&B features stylish rooms with modern comforts and a charming blend of rustic and contemporary decor. Guests can relax by the outdoor pool, explore the surrounding vineyards, and enjoy a homemade breakfast on the terrace. The warm hospitality and tranquil setting make it an ideal retreat for a peaceful getaway.

Gîtes du Mas Julianas

For a truly unique stay, consider Gîtes du Mas Julianas, a collection of self-catering cottages located in the picturesque countryside near Perpignan. These charming gîtes offer a home-away-from-home experience, with fully equipped kitchens, comfortable living areas, and private terraces. The property features a large garden, a swimming pool, and stunning views of the surrounding landscape. The friendly hosts provide a warm welcome and are happy to offer recommendations on local attractions and activities.

In conclusion, Perpignan offers a diverse range of accommodations to suit every traveller's needs and preferences. Whether you're seeking luxury, boutique charm, budget-friendly options, family-friendly stays, or unique lodging experiences, you'll find the perfect place to rest and rejuvenate during your visit to this vibrant city. Each accommodation option provides a different perspective on the city, allowing you to experience Perpignan's rich culture and hospitality in your unique way.

Chapter 4: Major Attractions

Perpignan is a city rich in history, culture, and beauty, offering a wide range of attractions that cater to all interests. From grand palaces and historic cathedrals to charming gardens and fascinating museums, there's no shortage of sights to see. This chapter explores five of Perpignan's most significant attractions, each offering a unique glimpse into the city's past and present.

Palais des Rois de Majorque

Historical Significance

The Palais des Rois de Majorque (Palace of the Kings of Majorca) is one of Perpignan's most iconic landmarks. Built in the late 13th century, this grand Gothic fortress served as the residence of the Kings of Majorca during their reign. The palace is a testament to the region's rich medieval history and the influence of the Majorcan kingdom.

Architectural Features

The palace is an architectural masterpiece, combining elements of Gothic and Romanesque styles. Its imposing walls and towers dominate the skyline, offering stunning views of the surrounding area. Inside, you'll find beautifully preserved halls, chapels, and courtyards, each showcasing intricate details and craftsmanship.

Visitor Experience

Visitors to the Palais des Rois de Majorque can explore the palace grounds, including the grand ceremonial rooms, the royal chapel, and the picturesque gardens. Guided tours are available, providing insights into the palace's history and significance. Don't miss the panoramic views from the towers, offering a breathtaking perspective of Perpignan and the surrounding countryside.

Perpignan Cathedral

Historical Background

Perpignan Cathedral, officially known as the Cathedral of Saint John the Baptist, is a magnificent example of Gothic architecture. Construction began in 1324 under King Sancho of Majorca and was completed in the 16th century. The cathedral has played a central role in the city's religious and cultural life for centuries.

Architectural Highlights

The cathedral's façade is a striking blend of Gothic and Baroque styles, featuring intricate stone carvings and a prominent rose window. Inside, you'll find a vast nave with soaring vaulted ceilings, beautiful stained glass windows, and an impressive high altar. The cathedral's chapels are adorned with exquisite artwork and religious relics.

Visitor Experience

A visit to Perpignan Cathedral offers a serene and contemplative experience. Take time to admire the stunning architecture, explore the various chapels, and learn about the cathedral's history through informative displays. The tranquil atmosphere provides a welcome respite from the bustling city outside.

Le Castillet

Historical Importance

Le Castillet is another of Perpignan's most recognizable landmarks. Originally built in the 14th century as a gatehouse and defensive structure, it later served as a prison. Today, it stands as a symbol of the city's medieval heritage and is home to the Casa Pairal Museum, which focuses on Catalan culture and history.

Architectural Features

Le Castillet's distinctive red brick façade and towering structure make it a prominent feature of Perpignan's cityscape. The building combines military and architectural elements, with its sturdy walls, crenellated parapets, and arched entranceways. Inside, the museum showcases a collection of artefacts, traditional costumes, and historical exhibits.

Visitor Experience

Visitors can explore the museum's exhibits to learn about the history and culture of Catalonia and Perpignan. The highlight of any visit is the climb to the top of Le Castillet, where you can enjoy panoramic views of the city and the surrounding region. The building's historical significance and unique architecture make it a must-see attraction.

Jardin de la Miranda

Overview

The Jardin de la Miranda is a beautiful public garden located in the heart of Perpignan. This green oasis offers a peaceful retreat from the city's hustle and bustle, with lush landscapes, vibrant flowerbeds, and tranquil pathways. It's a perfect spot for a stroll, a picnic, or simply relaxing in nature.

Features

The garden features a diverse collection of Mediterranean plants and flowers, creating a colourful and fragrant environment. Sculptures and fountains are scattered throughout, adding to the garden's charm. There are also shaded benches and seating areas where you can sit and enjoy the serene surroundings.

Visitor Experience

A visit to Jardin de la Miranda provides a refreshing break from sightseeing. Take a leisurely walk along the winding paths, admire the beautiful flora, and find a quiet spot to relax and unwind. The garden is also a popular spot for families, with plenty of space for children to play and explore.

Musée d'art Hyacinthe Rigaud

Historical Background

The Musée d'art Hyacinthe Rigaud is Perpignan's premier art museum, named after the famous portrait painter Hyacinthe Rigaud, who was born in the city. The museum is housed in two historic mansions, the Hôtel de Lazerme and the Hôtel de Mailly, which have been beautifully restored to showcase the museum's extensive collection.

Collections and Exhibits

The museum's collection spans several centuries, from the Renaissance to contemporary art. It includes works by renowned artists such as Hyacinthe Rigaud, Maillol, and Picasso. The exhibits feature a diverse range of paintings, sculptures, decorative arts, and temporary exhibitions that highlight different aspects of the region's artistic heritage.

Visitor Experience

Visitors to the Musée d'art Hyacinthe Rigaud can explore the museum's beautifully curated galleries, which are arranged thematically and chronologically. Informative displays and multimedia presentations provide context and insights into the artworks on display. The museum also offers educational programs, workshops, and guided tours, making it an enriching experience for art lovers of all ages.

Special Exhibitions

The museum regularly hosts special exhibitions, featuring works by both local and international artists. These exhibitions offer fresh perspectives and showcase a variety of artistic styles and mediums. Check the museum's calendar for current and upcoming exhibitions during your visit.

Museum Amenities

The Musée d'art Hyacinthe Rigaud provides a range of amenities to enhance your visit. There is a museum shop where you can purchase art books, prints, and souvenirs, as well as a café offering light refreshments and a pleasant spot to relax after exploring the galleries.

In conclusion, Perpignan's major attractions offer a fascinating glimpse into the city's rich history, culture, and artistic heritage. From the grandeur of the Palais des Rois de Majorque and the spiritual beauty of Perpignan Cathedral to the medieval charm of Le Castillet, the serene beauty of Jardin de la Miranda, and the artistic treasures of the Musée d'art Hyacinthe Rigaud, there is something for everyone to enjoy. Each of these attractions provides a unique and memorable experience, making your visit to Perpignan truly special.

Chapter 5: Exploring Neighborhoods

Perpignan is a city of diverse neighbourhoods, each with its unique charm and character. Exploring these areas provides a deeper understanding of the city's history, culture, and daily life. In this chapter, we will delve into four of Perpignan's most notable neighbourhoods: the Historic Center, Saint-Jacques, Les Remparts, and La Gare District.

The Historic Center

Overview

The Historic Center of Perpignan, also known as Le Centre Historique, is the heart of the city and a treasure trove of medieval and Renaissance architecture. This area is a labyrinth of narrow, winding streets lined with colourful buildings, charming squares, and historic landmarks.

Key Attractions

Le Castillet

Le Castillet, with its distinctive red brick façade, serves as the gateway to the Historic Center. This iconic structure, originally built as a fortress and later used as a prison, now houses the Casa Pairal Museum. Climb to the top for panoramic views of the city and explore the exhibits that showcase Perpignan's history and Catalan culture.

Perpignan Cathedral

Located in the heart of the Historic Center, Perpignan Cathedral is a must-visit. The Cathedral of Saint John the Baptist is an architectural gem with its Gothic and Baroque elements. Inside, you can admire the beautiful stained glass windows, the grand organ, and the intricately designed chapels.

Place de la Loge

This lively square is surrounded by some of Perpignan's most impressive buildings, including the Loge de Mer and the Town Hall. The square is a hub of activity, with outdoor cafés and shops offering a vibrant atmosphere. It's an ideal spot to relax and soak in the city's ambience.

Exploring the Streets

Wander through the maze of streets in the Historic Center to discover hidden gems, such as the Rue Paratilla, known for its food stalls and local delicacies. The area is also home to numerous boutiques, galleries, and artisanal shops, perfect for picking up unique souvenirs and gifts.

Saint-Jacques

Overview

Saint-Jacques is one of Perpignan's oldest and most culturally rich neighbourhoods. Traditionally known as a Romani and working-class district, Saint-Jacques is a melting pot of cultures and traditions. The area is characterized by its narrow streets, vibrant markets, and community spirit.

Key Attractions

Eglise Saint-Jacques

The Church of Saint James, or Eglise Saint-Jacques, is the focal point of the neighbourhood. This historic church dates back to the 14th century and features stunning Gothic architecture. It is particularly known for its beautiful bell tower and the annual Sanch procession during Holy Week.

Campo Santo

Adjacent to the Eglise Saint-Jacques is the Campo Santo, one of the oldest cemeteries in France. This peaceful and atmospheric site offers a unique glimpse into Perpignan's medieval past. The cemetery is also a venue for cultural events and concerts, adding to its allure.

Market Life

Saint-Jacques is renowned for its bustling markets, particularly the daily market at Place Cassanyes. Here, you can find a wide array of fresh produce, spices, textiles, and other goods. The market is a sensory delight, offering a vibrant slice of local life and a chance to interact with residents.

Cultural Diversity

The neighbourhood's multicultural character is reflected in its culinary offerings. From traditional Catalan cuisine to Moroccan and Romani dishes, Saint-Jacques is a food lover's paradise. Explore the local eateries and street food vendors to savour a diverse range of flavours.

Les Remparts

Overview

Les Remparts, or the Ramparts, is a district that reflects Perpignan's historical fortifications. This area is named after the city walls that once encircled Perpignan, remnants of which can still be seen today. Les Remparts offers a blend of history, culture, and green spaces.

Key Attractions
Jardin de la Miranda

One of the highlights of Les Remparts is the Jardin de la Miranda, a beautiful public garden that offers a serene escape from the city. This lush green space features Mediterranean plants, sculptures, and fountains. It's an ideal spot for a stroll or a picnic.

The City Walls
While much of the original city walls have been dismantled, several sections remain intact, providing a glimpse into Perpignan's defensive past. Walking along these remnants offers a unique perspective on the city's history and its strategic importance during medieval times.

Green Spaces
Les Remparts is home to several other parks and gardens, making it one of the greenest areas in Perpignan. The Parc Sant-Vicens is another popular spot, offering playgrounds, walking paths, and sports facilities. It's a great place for families and those looking to enjoy outdoor activities.

Residential Charm
The neighbourhood is primarily residential, with charming houses and quiet streets. It's a pleasant area to explore on foot, offering a peaceful contrast to the busier parts of the city. The local community is welcoming, and you'll often see residents enjoying the outdoor spaces and engaging in neighbourhood activities.

La Gare District

Overview

La Gare District, centred around Perpignan's main train station, is a bustling and dynamic area that serves as a gateway to the city. The district is a blend of modern conveniences and historical charm, with excellent transportation links and a vibrant local scene.

Key Attractions

Gare de Perpignan
The train station itself is an architectural landmark, famously described by Salvador Dalí as the "Center of the Universe." The station's Art Deco design and historical significance make it a point of interest. From here, you can catch trains to major cities in France and beyond, making it a convenient hub for travellers.

Place de Belgique
A short walk from the train station, Place de Belgique is a lively square surrounded by shops, cafés, and restaurants. The square often hosts events and markets, adding to the district's vibrant atmosphere. It's a great spot to people-watch and soak in the local culture.

Dining and Shopping

La Gare District offers a variety of dining options, from casual bistros to upscale restaurants. The area is known for its diverse culinary scene, reflecting Perpignan's multicultural influences. Whether you're in the mood for traditional French cuisine or international flavours, you'll find plenty of choices here.

Shopping enthusiasts will appreciate the district's array of boutiques and stores. From fashion to speciality shops, there's something for everyone. The proximity to the train station also means easy access to other parts of the city and the region.

Modern Conveniences

La Gare District is equipped with modern amenities, including hotels, car rental agencies, and tourist information centres. Its central location and excellent transport links make it a convenient base for exploring Perpignan and its surroundings.

Exploring Beyond Perpignan
The train station serves as a starting point for day trips to nearby towns and attractions. Whether you're heading to the beaches of the Mediterranean coast, the scenic villages in the Pyrenees, or the vibrant cities of Barcelona and Toulouse, La Gare District is your gateway to adventure.

In conclusion, Perpignan's neighbourhoods each offer a distinct experience, contributing to the city's rich tapestry of history, culture, and daily life. The Historic Center captivates with its medieval charm and iconic landmarks, Saint-Jacques enchants with its vibrant markets and cultural diversity, Les Remparts provides a peaceful retreat with its green spaces and historical remnants, and La Gare District buzzes with modern energy and connectivity. Exploring these neighbourhoods will deepen your appreciation of Perpignan's unique character and ensure a memorable visit.

Chapter 6: Cultural Experiences

Perpignan is a city that celebrates its rich cultural heritage with a vibrant array of festivals, performances, art galleries, and traditional music and dance. This chapter explores the diverse cultural experiences that make Perpignan a lively and dynamic destination.

Local Festivals and Events

La Sanch Procession

One of the most significant events in Perpignan is the La Sanch Procession, held during Holy Week. This ancient religious procession dates back to the 15th century and is a moving spectacle of faith and tradition. Participants, dressed in hooded robes, walk through the streets carrying statues of Christ and the Virgin Mary. The solemnity of the procession, accompanied by the mournful sounds of drums and chants, creates a powerful and evocative atmosphere.

Les Jeudis de Perpignan

Every summer, Perpignan comes alive with Les Jeudis de Perpignan, a series of free concerts and performances held every Thursday evening from June to September. These events feature a wide range of music genres, from jazz and classical to rock and traditional Catalan music. The city's squares and streets are transformed into open-air stages, creating a festive and communal atmosphere where locals and visitors can enjoy live music under the stars.

Visa pour l'Image

Perpignan is also known for its prestigious international photojournalism festival, Visa pour l'Image. Held annually in September, this festival attracts photographers, journalists, and photography enthusiasts from around the world. The event features powerful and thought-provoking photo exhibitions, workshops, and discussions, showcasing the best in contemporary photojournalism. Venues across the city, including historic buildings and public spaces, host these impactful displays, making it a citywide celebration of visual storytelling.

Fête de la Saint-Jean

The Fête de la Saint-Jean, or St. John's Day, is a traditional Catalan festival celebrated on June 23rd, marking the summer solstice. The festivities include bonfires, fireworks, and music, creating a lively and joyous atmosphere. One of the highlights is the lighting of the Canigou flame, which is carried from the peak of Mount Canigou to towns and villages across the region. In Perpignan, the flame is brought to the Place de la Loge, where the celebrations continue with dancing and revelry late into the night.

Theatre and Performances

Théâtre de l'Archipel

Théâtre de l'Archipel is Perpignan's premier cultural venue, offering a diverse program of theatre, dance, music, and contemporary performances. This modern theatre complex, designed by renowned architect Jean Nouvel, is an architectural marvel in itself. With its striking design and state-of-the-art facilities, Théâtre de l'Archipel hosts both local and international productions, providing a platform for artistic expression and creativity. The venue's varied program ensures that there is always something new and exciting to experience.

Le Médiator

Le Médiator is a popular live music venue in Perpignan, known for its eclectic lineup of concerts and performances.

From rock and pop to electronic and hip-hop, Le Médiator showcases a wide range of musical genres, attracting both local talent and renowned artists. The venue's intimate setting and excellent acoustics make it a favourite spot for music lovers. Check the schedule to see what's on during your visit, and immerse yourself in Perpignan's vibrant live music scene.

Théâtre Municipal

The Théâtre Municipal, located in the heart of the city, is a historic theatre that has been entertaining audiences since the 19th century. The theatre hosts a variety of performances, including plays, operas, ballets, and concerts. Its beautiful interior, adorned with ornate decorations and a grand chandelier, adds to the charm of attending a performance here. The Théâtre Municipal is a cultural landmark that continues to be a vital part of Perpignan's artistic life.

Art Galleries and Exhibitions

Musée d'art Hyacinthe Rigaud

The Musée d'art Hyacinthe Rigaud, named after the renowned portrait painter Hyacinthe Rigaud, is Perpignan's main art museum. The museum's extensive collection spans several centuries and includes works by notable artists such as Maillol, Picasso, and Dufy. The galleries are housed in two beautifully restored mansions, the Hôtel de Lazerme and the Hôtel de Mailly, which add to the museum's charm. The museum regularly hosts temporary exhibitions, showcasing contemporary art and thematic displays that offer fresh perspectives on its collections.

A Cent Mètres du Centre du Monde

A Cent Mètres du Centre du Monde is a contemporary art gallery located in a former industrial building near the train station. The gallery's name, which translates to "A Hundred Meters from the Center of the World," is inspired by Salvador Dalí's declaration about Perpignan's train station. This avant-garde space features rotating exhibitions of modern and contemporary art, highlighting both emerging and established artists. The gallery also hosts artist talks, workshops, and events, making it a dynamic hub for contemporary art in Perpignan.

Maison de la Catalanité

The Maison de la Catalanité is a cultural centre dedicated to promoting and preserving Catalan culture. The centre hosts a variety of exhibitions, events, and workshops that celebrate the region's artistic heritage. From traditional crafts and folk art to contemporary creations, the Maison de la Catalanité offers a comprehensive look at Catalan cultural expression. The centre also features a library and resource centre for those interested in learning more about Catalan history and traditions.

Traditional Music and Dance

Sardana

The Sardana is a traditional Catalan dance that is an integral part of Perpignan's cultural heritage. This circle dance, performed to the music of a cobla (a traditional Catalan band), is a symbol of unity and community. Sardana dancing is a common sight at festivals and public events, where people of all ages join hands and dance in circles. If you're visiting Perpignan during a local celebration, don't miss the opportunity to watch or even participate in this lively and joyful dance.

Cobla Music

Cobla music, characterized by the distinctive sound of instruments like the tenora and tible, is the traditional accompaniment for the Sardana dance. Cobla bands are often featured at local festivals and cultural events, providing a melodic backdrop for the dancing. The music is deeply rooted in Catalan culture and offers a unique auditory experience that reflects the region's traditions and spirit.

Rumba Catalana

Rumba Catalana is a vibrant genre of music that blends flamenco rhythms with Cuban and rock influences. Originating in the Catalan Romani communities, this lively music is characterized by its upbeat tempo, catchy melodies, and rhythmic guitar playing. Perpignan's bars and music venues often feature live Rumba Catalana performances, offering a lively and energetic atmosphere where you can enjoy this unique musical style.

Traditional Music Festivals

Perpignan hosts several music festivals throughout the year that celebrate traditional Catalan music and dance. The

Festival de Musique Sacrée, held in spring, focuses on sacred music from different cultures and traditions, featuring performances in historic venues across the city. The Estivales de Perpignan, a summer festival, includes a variety of concerts and cultural events, many of which highlight traditional Catalan music and dance. These festivals provide an excellent opportunity to experience the rich musical heritage of the region.

In conclusion, Perpignan offers a wealth of cultural experiences that reflect its rich history and vibrant traditions. From local festivals and theatre performances to art galleries and traditional music and dance, there is always something to inspire and engage visitors. Exploring these cultural offerings will deepen your appreciation of Perpignan's unique character and ensure a memorable and enriching stay in this dynamic city.

Chapter 7: Outdoor Adventures

Perpignan, nestled between the Mediterranean Sea and the Pyrenees Mountains, offers a playground of outdoor adventures for nature enthusiasts and active travellers alike. This chapter explores the diverse range of outdoor activities available in and around the city.

Hiking and Nature Trails

Les Orgues d'Ille-sur-Têt

Les Orgues d'Ille-sur-Têt, located just a short drive from Perpignan, is a unique natural site renowned for its towering rock formations. These organ-pipe-shaped columns, formed by erosion over thousands of years, create a striking landscape that is perfect for hiking and exploration. Several well-marked trails lead through the rock formations, offering stunning views of the surrounding countryside and opportunities for photography.

Pic du Canigou

For more adventurous hikers, Pic du Canigou offers a challenging ascent and breathtaking panoramic views. This iconic peak, part of the Pyrenees range, stands at 2,784 meters and is considered sacred by the Catalan people. The hike to the summit takes approximately six to eight hours, depending on the route chosen, and rewards hikers with spectacular vistas of the Pyrenees, the Mediterranean Sea, and the surrounding valleys.

La Massane

Closer to Perpignan, La Massane is a popular hiking destination that offers a moderate climb and scenic views. The trail winds through forests of cork oak and chestnut trees, leading to the summit at 1,056 meters. From the top, hikers can enjoy panoramic views of the Mediterranean coastline and the Albères Mountains. The hike typically takes around three to four hours round-trip, making it ideal for a half-day adventure.

Beaches and Water Activities

Canet-en-Roussillon

Canet-en-Roussillon, just a short drive from Perpignan, boasts some of the region's most beautiful beaches. The long sandy shores and clear blue waters make it an ideal spot for sunbathing, swimming, and water sports. Canet Plage is a family-friendly beach with amenities such as beach clubs, restaurants, and water sports rentals. For those seeking a quieter experience, the nearby natural reserve of Étang de Canet-Saint-Nazaire offers tranquil beaches and opportunities for birdwatching.

Collioure

Further south along the coast, Collioure is a picturesque seaside town known for its vibrant colours, historic charm, and scenic beaches. The town's rocky coves and clear waters are perfect for snorkelling, paddleboarding, and kayaking. Collioure's beaches, such as Plage de Saint-Vincent and Plage Boramar, offer a mix of sandy stretches and rocky outcrops, ideal for both relaxing and exploring underwater marine life.

Cycling Routes

Voie Verte

The Voie Verte, or Greenway, is a scenic cycling route that follows the path of a former railway line from Perpignan to Thuir. This flat and well-maintained route is suitable for cyclists of all levels and offers picturesque views of vineyards, orchards, and rural landscapes. Along the way, cyclists can stop at charming villages, such as Elne and Ponteilla, to explore local markets, cafes, and historical sites.

Coastal Cycling
Cycling enthusiasts can explore the scenic coastal paths that stretch along the Mediterranean Sea. From Perpignan, cyclists can ride south towards Argelès-sur-Mer and Collioure, passing by sandy beaches, rocky coves, and seaside villages. The coastal route offers stunning views of the Mediterranean coastline and opportunities to stop for picnics or swimming in secluded spots.

Parks and Gardens

Jardin de la Miranda
Located within Perpignan's Les Remparts district, Jardin de la Miranda is a peaceful oasis featuring Mediterranean flora, sculptures, and shaded pathways. The garden's tranquil ambience makes it an ideal spot for a stroll, picnic, or relaxation amidst nature. The garden also offers panoramic views of Perpignan's historic city walls and surrounding countryside.

Parc Sant-Vicens
Parc Sant-Vicens, situated in Perpignan's Les Remparts district, is a family-friendly park with playgrounds, walking trails, and sports facilities. The park's spacious lawns and wooded areas provide ample space for outdoor activities such

as jogging, cycling, and picnicking. Parc Sant-Vicens is a popular spot for residents to unwind and enjoy nature in the heart of the city.

Promenade de la Côte Vermeille
Stretching along the coast near Collioure, the Promenade de la Côte Vermeille offers a scenic walkway with panoramic views of the Mediterranean Sea and rocky coastline. This coastal path is lined with palm trees, flowering shrubs, and benches, making it perfect for a stroll or jogging with stunning sea views. The promenade also connects to several secluded beaches and coves, where visitors can relax and swim in crystal-clear waters.

In conclusion, Perpignan and its surrounding region offer a diverse array of outdoor adventures for nature lovers and outdoor enthusiasts. Whether you prefer hiking through rugged landscapes, relaxing on sandy beaches, exploring scenic cycling routes, or enjoying tranquil parks and gardens, there's something for everyone to enjoy amidst the natural beauty of this captivating region.

Chapter 8: Culinary Delights

Perpignan's culinary scene is a reflection of its rich Catalan heritage, blending traditional flavours with modern influences. This chapter explores the city's gastronomic offerings, from traditional Catalan cuisine to top restaurants, street food, markets, and local wineries.

Traditional Catalan Cuisine

Fruits de Mer

Perpignan's proximity to the Mediterranean Sea ensures a bounty of fresh seafood, which plays a central role in Catalan cuisine. Local specialities include anchovies marinated in vinegar (anxoves), grilled sardines (sardines a la plancha), and seafood paella (paella de mariscos). These dishes highlight the region's maritime flavours and are often enjoyed with a glass of crisp white wine.

Escudella i Carn d'Olla

Escudella i Carn d'Olla is a hearty Catalan stew that is traditionally served during festive occasions and family gatherings. The stew features a variety of meats, such as pork, chicken, and sausage, simmered with vegetables and chickpeas. It's a comforting dish that reflects Catalan culinary traditions and is best enjoyed with crusty bread and aioli.

Crema Catalana

No culinary journey through Catalonia is complete without tasting Crema Catalana, a delicious dessert similar to crème brûlée. This creamy custard is flavoured with vanilla and citrus zest and then caramelized on top to create a crispy, sugary crust. It's a perfect way to end a traditional Catalan meal and is often paired with a glass of sweet Muscat wine.

Top Restaurants

Le Divil

Le Divil is a Michelin-starred restaurant located in Perpignan's historic centre, known for its innovative approach to Catalan cuisine. Chef David Gomez creates dishes that celebrate local ingredients with a contemporary twist. The restaurant's elegant ambience and impeccable service make it a popular choice for special occasions and gourmet dining experiences.

La Galinette

La Galinette offers a refined dining experience with a focus on fresh, seasonal ingredients sourced from local producers. Located in a charming townhouse in Perpignan, the restaurant showcases traditional Catalan flavours in dishes such as grilled seafood, roasted meats, and creative vegetable preparations. The intimate atmosphere and attentive service ensure a memorable meal.

L'Alchimiste

L'Alchimiste is celebrated for its creative cuisine and stylish setting, combining traditional Catalan recipes with modern culinary techniques. The restaurant's menu features dishes that highlight the region's seasonal bounty, from artisanal cheeses and charcuterie to inventive desserts. With a diverse wine list showcasing local and international selections, L'Alchimiste offers a gastronomic journey through Perpignan's culinary landscape.

Street Food and Markets

Place de la République Market

Place de la République hosts a bustling market every Saturday morning, where local vendors offer a vibrant array of fresh produce, cheeses, meats, and seafood. Visitors can sample regional specialities such as olives marinated in herbs (olives cassées), cured meats (charcuterie), and freshly baked pastries (pâtisseries). The market is also a great place to purchase artisanal products and souvenirs.

Food Trucks and Stands

Perpignan's streets come alive with food trucks and stand offering quick and delicious bites inspired by Catalan and international flavors. From savoury crepes (galettes) filled with cheese and ham to grilled Catalan sausages (butifarra), there's a wide variety of street food to satisfy every palate. These mobile eateries are perfect for grabbing a quick lunch or sampling local specialities on the go.

Local Wineries and Vineyards

Domaine Lafage

Domaine Lafage is a renowned winery located just outside Perpignan, known for producing high-quality wines that showcase the region's terroir. The winery offers guided tours and tastings where visitors can sample a range of wines, from crisp whites made with local Grenache Blanc to robust reds crafted from old-vine Carignan. The scenic vineyards provide a picturesque backdrop for learning about winemaking traditions in Catalonia.

Domaine de Rombeau

Domaine de Rombeau, nestled in the Roussillon wine region near Perpignan, is a family-owned winery with a legacy dating back several generations. The estate produces a diverse selection of wines, including aromatic Muscats, elegant Grenaches, and fortified Banyuls wines. Visitors can explore the vineyards, tour the cellar, and enjoy tastings paired with local cheeses and charcuterie, immersing themselves in the flavours of Catalonia.

Mas Janeil

Mas Janeil is a boutique winery known for its organic and biodynamic approach to winemaking, producing terroir-driven wines that reflect the unique characteristics of the Roussillon region. The winery's vineyards, situated in the foothills of the Pyrenees Mountains, benefit from a Mediterranean climate and mineral-rich soils, ideal for cultivating expressive wines. Guided tours and tastings at Mas Janeil offer a personalized experience, highlighting sustainable practices and artisanal craftsmanship.

In conclusion, Perpignan's culinary scene is a feast for the senses, showcasing the best of Catalan cuisine, top-notch restaurants, vibrant markets, and prestigious wineries. Whether you're savouring traditional dishes, dining at Michelin-starred establishments, exploring street food delights, or tasting wines at local vineyards, you'll discover a culinary landscape rich in flavour, history, and culture. Enjoying these culinary delights is an essential part of experiencing the vibrant gastronomy of Perpignan and its surrounding region.

Chapter 9: Shopping Experiences

Exploring Perpignan's shopping scene is a delightful way to immerse yourself in the local culture and discover unique treasures. This chapter guides you through the city's diverse shopping experiences, from vibrant markets and charming artisan shops to bustling shopping streets and malls.

Local Markets

Place de la République Market
The Place de la République Market is a bustling hub of activity, held every Saturday morning in Perpignan's historic centre. This lively market features a wide array of stalls offering fresh produce, cheeses, meats, seafood, and local specialities. It's a great place to sample Catalan delicacies such as olives marinated in herbs (olives cassées), cured meats

(charcuterie), and artisanal cheeses. The market also boasts handicrafts, textiles, and souvenirs, making it perfect for browsing and discovering authentic Catalan flavours and goods.

Marché Saint-Charles
Marché Saint-Charles is another popular market in Perpignan, open daily except Mondays. Located near the railway station, this covered market is a treasure trove of fresh fruits, vegetables, meats, cheeses, and seafood sourced from local producers. Visitors can shop for picnic supplies, gourmet treats, and regional specialities while soaking in the vibrant atmosphere and mingling with locals.

Shopping Streets and Malls

Rue de la Loge
Rue de la Loge is Perpignan's main shopping street, lined with a mix of upscale boutiques, international brands, and local shops. This pedestrian-friendly thoroughfare invites shoppers to explore its fashion boutiques, jewellery stores, artisanal crafts shops, and speciality stores. Whether you're searching for the latest trends or unique gifts, Rue de la Loge offers a diverse shopping experience in the heart of the city.

Centre Commercial Le Polygone
For a modern shopping experience, head to Centre Commercial Le Polygone, Perpignan's largest shopping mall located near the city centre. This mall features a wide range of stores, including fashion retailers, electronics shops, home goods stores, and beauty boutiques. Visitors can also enjoy

dining options, cinemas, and entertainment facilities, making it a convenient destination for shopping and leisure activities under one roof.

Unique Souvenirs

Catalan Ceramics

Catalan ceramics are renowned for their vibrant colours and intricate designs, reflecting the region's artistic heritage. Look for handcrafted pottery, decorative tiles, and kitchenware adorned with traditional motifs such as Mediterranean landscapes, floral patterns, and geometric shapes. Artisan workshops and boutiques in Perpignan offer a selection of ceramic souvenirs that make memorable gifts and keepsakes from your visit.

Perfumes and Cosmetics

Perpignan is home to several perfumeries and cosmetics shops that specialize in creating fragrances and skincare products inspired by the region's natural ingredients. Explore boutique perfumeries to discover locally made perfumes, body oils, soaps, and lotions infused with floral essences, herbal extracts, and citrus notes. These aromatic treasures capture the essence of Catalonia and make luxurious souvenirs to cherish.

Artisan Shops

Ateliers d'Art

Ateliers d'Art, or artisan workshops, are scattered throughout Perpignan's historic neighbourhoods, offering a glimpse into traditional craftsmanship and contemporary artistry. Visit studios specializing in woodworking, glassblowing, jewellery making, and textile arts to witness artisans at work and purchase handmade creations. These artisan shops provide unique opportunities to acquire one-of-a-kind pieces that embody Perpignan's creative spirit and cultural heritage.

La Maison de la Catalanité
La Maison de la Catalanité is a cultural centre and shop dedicated to promoting Catalan traditions and craftsmanship. Browse a curated collection of artisanal products, including textiles, ceramics, jewellery, and gourmet foods, sourced from local artisans and producers. This cultural hub also hosts exhibitions, workshops, and events that celebrate Catalan culture, providing an enriching shopping experience rooted in authenticity and creativity.

In conclusion, Perpignan offers a rich tapestry of shopping experiences that cater to every taste and interest, from exploring vibrant markets and chic shopping streets to discovering unique souvenirs and artisanal crafts. Whether you're indulging in local delicacies at bustling markets, exploring fashion boutiques on Rue de la Loge, or discovering handmade treasures in artisan workshops, shopping in Perpignan promises to be a memorable and rewarding adventure. Embrace the city's vibrant shopping scene to bring home a piece of Catalan culture and create lasting memories of your visit to this dynamic destination.

Chapter 10: Day Trips

Perpignan's strategic location offers easy access to a variety of captivating destinations within Catalonia and beyond. This chapter explores four enriching day trips that highlight the region's cultural heritage, natural beauty, and picturesque landscapes.

Collioure

Overview
Just a short drive south of Perpignan lies the charming seaside town of Collioure, renowned for its stunning coastal scenery,

vibrant art scene, and historic charm. Collioure's distinctive architecture, colourful buildings, and scenic beaches have long inspired artists such as Matisse and Derain, who were captivated by its unique light and Mediterranean ambience.

Things to Do
Explore the picturesque streets lined with art galleries, boutiques, and cafes.
Visit the Royal Castle (Château Royal) overlooking the sea, which offers panoramic views of the town and coastline.
Relax on Collioure's sandy beaches or swim in the crystal-clear waters of the Mediterranean Sea.
Discover local Catalan cuisine at seaside restaurants, specializing in fresh seafood and regional dishes.
Browse the vibrant local market (Wednesdays and Sundays) for artisan crafts, fresh produce, and souvenirs.

Travel Tips
Collioure is approximately a 30-minute drive from Perpignan, making it an ideal day trip destination.
Parking can be limited in the town centre, especially during peak tourist seasons, so arrive early if possible.
Consider visiting during the quieter shoulder seasons (spring or autumn) to avoid crowds and enjoy a more relaxed experience.

Céret

Overview
Nestled in the foothills of the Pyrenees Mountains, Céret is a picturesque town renowned for its artistic heritage, lively atmosphere, and scenic surroundings. It has long been a magnet for artists drawn to its beautiful light and natural beauty, earning it the nickname "City of Cherries" due to its abundant orchards.

Things to Do
Explore the Musée d'Art Moderne, home to a renowned collection of modern art and works by Picasso, Chagall, and other masters.
Stroll through Céret's charming streets lined with art galleries, boutiques, and cafes.
Visit the colourful Saturday market, where local vendors sell fresh produce, cheeses, olives, and handmade crafts.
Hike or cycle in the nearby hills and forests, which offer scenic trails and panoramic views of the Pyrenees.
Sample local delicacies such as cherry-based products, wines from nearby vineyards, and traditional Catalan dishes.

Travel Tips
Céret is approximately a 40-minute drive from Perpignan, passing through picturesque countryside and vineyards.

The town's compact size makes it easy to explore on foot, but wear comfortable shoes as some streets are cobblestoned. Check local event calendars for festivals and cultural events, which often showcase music, dance, and traditional Catalan celebrations.

Castelnou

Overview

Nestled in the foothills of the Pyrenees Mountains, Castelnou is a picturesque medieval village that exudes charm and history. Surrounded by vineyards and olive groves, this fortified village is known for its well-preserved medieval architecture, narrow cobblestone streets, and panoramic views of the Roussillon plains.

Things to Do
Explore the winding streets of Castelnou, lined with medieval houses, artisan workshops, and traditional Catalan boutiques.
Visit the Château de Castelnou, a medieval castle offering guided tours that provide insights into the village's history and architecture.
Admire panoramic views of the surrounding countryside from the village's hilltop location.
Sample local wines and olive oils at tastings offered by vineyards and producers in the area.
Enjoy a leisurely meal at one of Castelnou's charming restaurants, offering traditional Catalan cuisine and regional specialities.

Travel Tips
Castelnou is approximately a 45-minute drive from Perpignan, passing through scenic countryside and vineyards.
Parking is available outside the village, as Castelnou's narrow streets are pedestrian-only, allowing for a peaceful and atmospheric visit.
Visit during the spring or autumn to experience mild weather and fewer tourists, enhancing your exploration of this historic village.

The Pyrenees Mountains

Overview
For nature enthusiasts and outdoor adventurers, the Pyrenees Mountains offer a breathtaking backdrop for exploration, hiking, and scenic drives. Stretching along the border between France and Spain, this mountain range is characterized by rugged peaks, verdant valleys, pristine lakes, and diverse wildlife.

Things to Do
Embark on a scenic drive through the Pyrenees, following winding roads that offer panoramic views of mountain vistas, alpine meadows, and picturesque villages.
Explore hiking trails that range from leisurely walks to challenging climbs, allowing you to discover cascading waterfalls, ancient forests, and stunning viewpoints.
Visit mountain lakes such as Lac des Bouillouses or Lac de Matemale, where you can enjoy picnics, fishing, and water sports amidst breathtaking natural scenery.

Experience winter sports such as skiing, snowboarding, and snowshoeing at ski resorts such as Font-Romeu, Les Angles, or La Molina.

Discover charming mountain villages and towns, each offering unique cultural heritage, traditional cuisine, and opportunities to connect with residents.

Travel Tips

The Pyrenees Mountains are easily accessible from Perpignan by car, with numerous scenic routes and mountain passes to explore.

Plan your visit according to seasonal activities, with winter offering snow sports and summer providing opportunities for hiking, wildlife watching, and outdoor adventures.

Pack appropriate clothing and gear based on your chosen activities, as mountain weather can vary and change rapidly.

In conclusion, Perpignan's proximity to diverse destinations allows travellers to experience the best of Catalonia's cultural heritage, natural beauty, and outdoor adventures on enriching day trips. Whether you're exploring the coastal charm of Collioure, immersing yourself in Céret's artistic atmosphere, discovering the medieval village of Castelnou, or venturing into the scenic Pyrenees Mountains, each day trip promises unforgettable experiences and insights into this dynamic region. Enjoy exploring these captivating destinations from your base in Perpignan, creating lasting memories of your journey through Catalonia's diverse landscapes and cultural treasures.

Chapter 11: Practical Information

Visiting Perpignan requires practical considerations to ensure a smooth and enjoyable experience. This chapter provides essential information on currency, language tips, safety, health, internet connectivity, and emergency contacts to help you navigate your journey with confidence.

Currency and Money Matters

Perpignan, like the rest of France, uses the Euro (EUR, €) as its official currency. ATMs (Distributeurs Automatiques de Billets) are widely available throughout the city, allowing you to withdraw cash using major credit and debit cards. Credit cards such as Visa and MasterCard are widely accepted in shops, restaurants, and hotels. It's advisable to carry some cash for smaller purchases and transactions in markets or local establishments.

Language Tips

The official language spoken in Perpignan and the wider region of Catalonia is French. However, due to its proximity to Spain and Catalan cultural influences, Catalan is also spoken by some residents. Basic French phrases can be useful for everyday interactions, though many locals also speak English, especially in tourist areas. Learning a few common phrases in French or Catalan can enhance your experience and communication with locals.

Safety and Health

Perpignan is generally a safe destination for travellers, but it's essential to take common-sense precautions. Keep an eye on your belongings in crowded places and avoid displaying large sums of money or valuable items. Emergency services in France can be reached by dialling 112 for police, ambulance, or fire emergencies. Medical services are accessible through hospitals, clinics, and pharmacies throughout the city.

Internet and Connectivity

Staying connected in Perpignan is convenient, with many hotels, cafes, and restaurants offering free Wi-Fi for guests. SIM cards with data plans can be purchased from local mobile providers for those needing constant internet access on their mobile devices. Additionally, Perpignan has public Wi-Fi hotspots in some public spaces, providing connectivity for tourists and residents alike.

Emergency Contacts

- Emergency Services: Dial 112 for police, ambulance, or fire emergencies.
- Police: For non-emergency assistance or reporting incidents, you can contact the local police station
- Medical Assistance: For medical emergencies, hospitals and clinics in Perpignan provide 24-hour services.

In conclusion, understanding these practical aspects of visiting Perpignan will ensure a seamless experience, allowing you to focus on enjoying the city's rich culture, historic landmarks, and culinary delights. By familiarizing yourself with currency exchange, language nuances, safety measures, health services, internet access, and emergency contacts, you can navigate Perpignan with confidence and make the most of your travels in this captivating destination.

Chapter 12: Travel Tips

Planning a trip to Perpignan involves considering various factors to enhance your experience and make your journey memorable. This chapter provides essential travel tips, including the best times to visit, packing suggestions, eco-friendly travel practices, and local etiquette, ensuring you're well-prepared for your adventure in Perpignan.

Best Times to Visit

Perpignan enjoys a Mediterranean climate, characterized by mild winters and hot summers, making it a year-round destination. However, the best times to visit depend on your preferences and the activities you plan to enjoy:

- Spring (April to June): Ideal for mild weather, blooming landscapes, and fewer tourists. It's perfect for exploring outdoor attractions and attending local festivals.

- Summer (July to August): Peak tourist season with hot temperatures and a lively atmosphere. Ideal for beachgoers and outdoor activities, though expect more crowds and higher prices.

- Autumn (September to October): Pleasant temperatures, fewer tourists, and vibrant autumn colours. It's a great time for cultural events, wine tasting, and hiking in nearby mountains.

- Winter (November to March): Mild temperatures but cooler than other seasons. It's quieter with fewer tourists, ideal for exploring indoor attractions, enjoying local cuisine, and experiencing Christmas markets.

Consider seasonal events and your preferred weather conditions when planning your visit to Perpignan.

Essential Packing List

Packing essentials for your trip to Perpignan:
- Lightweight clothing: Pack comfortable clothing suitable for warm temperatures, including shorts, t-shirts, and summer dresses for the summer months. Bring layers for cooler evenings during spring and autumn.

- Sun protection: Sunscreen, sunglasses, and a wide-brimmed hat to protect against strong Mediterranean sun.

- Comfortable shoes: Walking shoes or sandals for exploring cobblestone streets and hiking trails.

- Swimwear: If visiting during summer, pack swimwear for beach visits or hotel pools.

- Travel adapter: French electrical outlets typically use Type E sockets. Bring a universal adapter if needed.

- Medications: Personal medications and a small first aid kit for minor injuries or ailments.

- Reusable water bottle: Stay hydrated and reduce plastic waste by carrying a reusable water bottle.

- Travel guides and maps: Although digital resources are available, having a physical guidebook or map can help navigate the city and its surroundings.

Eco-Friendly Travel Practices

Promote sustainable travel practices during your visit to Perpignan:

- Use public transportation: Opt for buses or trains to reduce carbon emissions and support local transit systems.

- Choose eco-friendly accommodations: Stay in hotels or guesthouses that prioritize sustainability initiatives, such as energy efficiency and waste reduction.

- Reduce plastic use: Carry a reusable shopping bag and water bottle. Refuse single-use plastics when dining or shopping.

- Respect natural surroundings: Stay on designated trails when hiking, avoid disturbing wildlife, and dispose of waste responsibly.

- Support local businesses: Shop at local markets, dine at restaurants using locally sourced ingredients and purchase souvenirs crafted by local artisans.

By adopting eco-friendly practices, you can minimize your environmental footprint and contribute positively to Perpignan's preservation and community well-being.

Local Etiquette

Understanding local customs and etiquette enhances cultural immersion and fosters respectful interactions with residents:

- Greetings: Begin conversations with a polite greeting, such as "Bonjour" (Good day) or "Bonsoir" (Good evening). Use formal titles (Monsieur/Madame) when addressing strangers.

- Dining etiquette: When dining out, wait to be seated and use utensils rather than eating with hands. It's customary to linger over meals and enjoy multiple courses.

- Language: While French is the official language, some locals also speak Catalan. Learning basic French phrases can show respect and facilitate communication.

- Tipping: Tipping is appreciated but not obligatory in France. A service charge is often included in the bill, but leaving a small additional tip for exceptional service is customary.

- Respect cultural sites: When visiting churches, museums, or historic sites, dress modestly and observe any posted rules or guidelines.

By embracing local etiquette and customs, you'll create meaningful connections with locals and enrich your cultural experience in Perpignan.

In conclusion, these travel tips provide valuable insights to help you plan and enjoy your visit to Perpignan. Whether you're exploring historic landmarks, indulging in local cuisine, or immersing yourself in the region's natural beauty, preparation ensures a memorable and rewarding journey. Embrace the city's Mediterranean charm, adopt eco-friendly practices, and respect local customs to make the most of your travels in this captivating destination.

Chapter 13: Conclusion

As your journey through Perpignan draws to a close, reflect on the city's captivating charm, rich history, and vibrant culture. This concluding chapter summarizes Perpignan's highlights, offers tips for a memorable visit, and bids farewell while suggesting possibilities for future adventures in this enchanting destination.

Summary of Perpignan's Highlights

Perpignan, nestled in the heart of Catalan culture, invites travellers to explore its diverse attractions and experiences:

- Historic Landmarks: Discover medieval treasures such as Palais des Rois de Majorque and Le Castillet, showcasing the city's architectural splendour and royal legacy.

- Cultural Experiences: Immerse yourself in local festivals, art galleries, and traditional music, celebrating Perpignan's artistic vibrancy and Catalan heritage.

- Outdoor Adventures: From hiking in the Pyrenees Mountains to relaxing on Mediterranean beaches, Perpignan offers diverse landscapes for nature enthusiasts and adventurers alike.

- Culinary Delights: Indulge in traditional Catalan cuisine, savouring fresh seafood, local wines, and street food delights that reflect the region's culinary diversity.

Tips for a Memorable Visit

Make the most of your stay in Perpignan with these practical tips:

- Plan Ahead: Research seasonal events and activities to tailor your visit to personal interests, whether it's attending festivals or exploring outdoor adventures.

- Embrace Local Culture: Learn a few French or Catalan phrases to connect with locals and enhance cultural exchanges.

- Explore Beyond Perpignan: Take day trips to charming towns like Collioure, Céret, and Castelnou, or venture into the Pyrenees Mountains for scenic vistas and outdoor activities.

- Savour Every Moment: Slow down, enjoy leisurely meals, and soak in the ambience of Perpignan's historic streets, markets, and cultural venues.

Farewell and Future Visits

As you bid farewell to Perpignan, consider future visits to further explore its hidden gems, seasonal offerings, and evolving cultural scene. Whether returning to witness festivals, indulge in culinary delights, or simply unwind amidst Mediterranean landscapes, Perpignan welcomes you with open arms for future adventures and discoveries.

Reflect on the memories made, the friendships forged, and the beauty of Perpignan that has left an indelible mark on your journey. Until we meet again in this enchanting corner of Catalonia, may your travels be filled with joy, discovery, and a renewed appreciation for the magic of Perpignan.

In closing, Perpignan beckons with its blend of history, culture, and natural beauty—a city where every visit unveils new wonders and enriching experiences. Cherish the moments shared and carry the spirit of Perpignan with you as you continue your travels, knowing that its vibrant charm awaits your return.

This conclusion encapsulates the essence of Perpignan, offering a fond farewell while leaving open the possibility for future explorations in this captivating city and its surroundings.

Chapter 14: Appendix

Explore additional resources and practical information to enhance your experience in Perpignan. This appendix provides maps, language tips, recommended reading, and an index for quick reference during your visit.

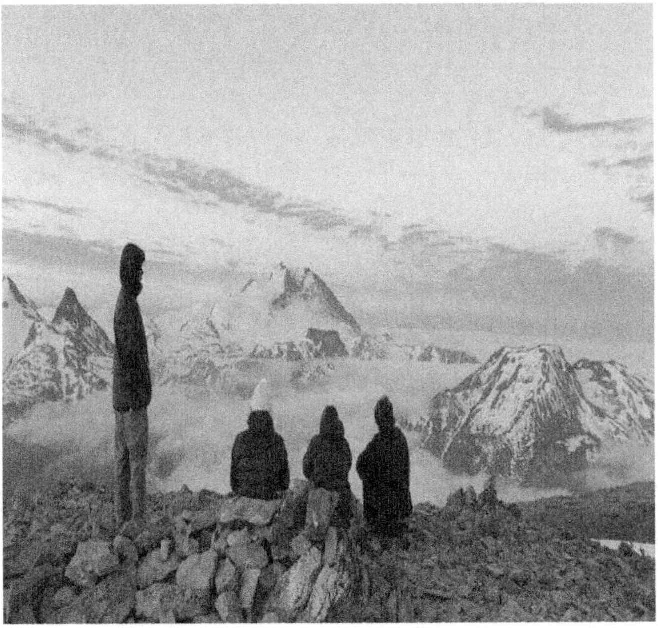

Maps of Perpignan

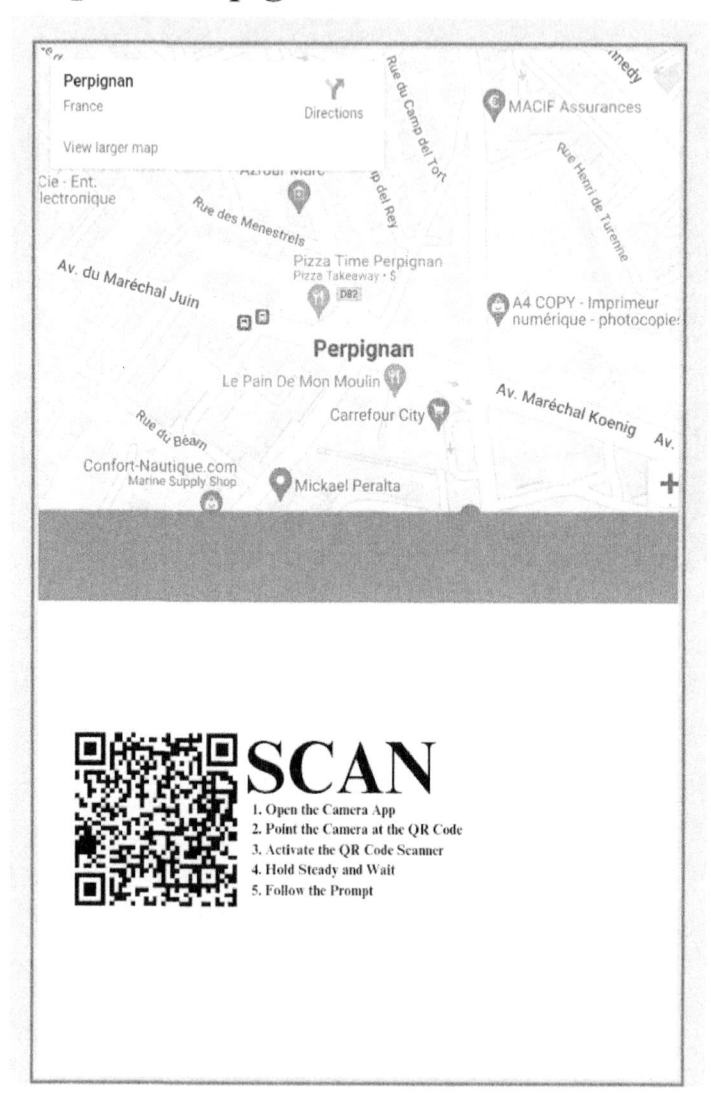

SCAN
1. Open the Camera App
2. Point the Camera at the QR Code
3. Activate the QR Code Scanner
4. Hold Steady and Wait
5. Follow the Prompt

Useful Phrases in French and Catalan

French Phrases

- Bonjour - Good morning/Hello
- Bonsoir - Good evening
- Merci - Thank you
- S'il vous plaît - Please
- Où est...? - Where is...?
- L'addition, s'il vous plaît - The bill, please

Catalan Phrases

- Bon dia - Good morning
- Bona tarda - Good afternoon
- Gràcies - Thank you
- Per favour - Please
- On és...? - Where is...?
- La compta, si us plau - The bill, please

Recommended Reading and Resources

Books

- The Art of Perpignan by Jean-Pierre Servais: Explore the city's artistic heritage and architectural wonders through this comprehensive guide.

- Catalan Cuisine: A Culinary Journey through Catalonia by Maria Josep Casas: Discover the flavours and traditions of Catalan cuisine, including Perpignan's culinary delights.

Websites

- Perpignan Tourism Official Website: www.perpignantourisme.com - Provides up-to-date information on attractions, events, and practical travel tips.

- Lonely Planet Perpignan Guide: www.lonelyplanet.com/perpignan - Offers insights, recommendations, and traveller reviews to plan your visit effectively.

Index

Quickly locate information within this guide using the index, which lists key topics, attractions, and practical tips covered throughout the chapters.

This appendix serves as a valuable resource, offering maps for navigation, language tips for communication, recommended reading for deeper insights, and an index for easy reference during your exploration of Perpignan. Enjoy your journey through this vibrant city and the cultural riches it offers.

**THANK YOU!
HAVE A NICE
JOURNEY!!**

Printed in Great Britain
by Amazon